bush
PUBLISHING
& associates

PRAISE *Matters*

Scriptures to inspire, bless and encourage.

J.M. SMITH

Discover the difference
that praise can make in your life

bush
PUBLISHING
& associates

Praise Matters

ISBN 978-1-7375981-9-0
ISBN 979-8-9854481-1-5

Printed in the United States of America.

First printing 2021 by Bush Publishing and Associates, LLC
Tulsa, Oklahoma
www.bushpublishing.com

Bush Publishing & Associates, LLC books may be ordered at bookstores everywhere and at Amazon.com.

Cover Art by Sarah Loehr.

Layout and Design by Bush Publishing and Associates, LLC, Tulsa, OK.

Editing by Writing By Michele, LLC, Tulsa, OK.

All opinions expressed in this book are the author's.

This book is dedicated to the memory of

ADDYSON (ADDY) MAY

March 19–29, 2012

I will turn their mourning into joy. I will comfort them
and exchange their sorrow for rejoicing.

Jeremiah 31:13 (NLT)

A heartbreak that challenged my faith,
inspired this book, and
transformed my life.

*We cannot be too firm
in the holy resolve to praise God,
for it is the chief end of our living and being
that we should glorify God
and enjoy Him forever.*

Charles Haddon Spurgeon (1834–1892)

Introduction

My decision to pursue a life of praise was born out of a deep hurt that sent my faith reeling. My world shifted for a moment and I almost lost my footing. Enveloped in grief and hounded by doubt, my prayers and litany of questions remained unanswered. Eventually I was prompted to reread Don Gossett's book, *There's Dynamite in Praise*.

As I went deeper into the book, something he said resonated with me:

"When all else fails, praise prevails. Human persuasion, begging with tears, and all else often fails to produce anticipated results. But praise never fails to bring God's response to us..."

And why does praise prevail, I wondered?

"Because God inhabits our praises!" For *"...praise is the language of faith, and faith is the victory."*[1]

Eager to know more, I read on. When I got to Brother Gossett's chapter on "One Hundred Praise Scriptures," I was inspired to do my own study. Concordance in hand, I came up with a list of more than 100 Scriptures related to praise and thanksgiving.

The result is this little book. And even though I did not receive the answers I thought I so desperately needed, I discovered something infinitely better: **Giving praise freed me from having to understand everything.**

As I made my way through the valley of the shadow of death, praise was the walking stick that kept me from stumbling. And on the other side I found my faith ignited, my heart healed, and my confidence in God restored. Hallelujah!

I challenge you to begin your own praise journey and "…*offer the sacrifice of praise to God, that is, the fruit of our lips, giving thanks to His name*"—Hebrews 13:15 (NKJV). Go ahead, whisper your words of praise; speak them out loud; sing them; shout them; meditate on them throughout the day. Purpose in your heart to do this when you're sad and worn out; when you're happy and everything is going well; when you're weak and you feel like quitting… and *especially* when the most difficult thing to do is praise.

My hope is that this book will inspire you to begin a life of praise, and begin it *now*. Regardless of all that may be wrong in your life, in spite of the way you feel, you *can* choose to be thankful for past and present blessings and, in faith, look forward to God's promises for the future.

Take that first step in making praise an essential part of your daily life, the driving force to discovering that" *praise is so harmonious with God's expectation of us that it is the power that makes our lives fragrant with heaven's best.*"[2]

Blessings and joy!

Janet

If you only knew what happens in the spirit
when you rejoice,
you would rejoice every day!

Mark Hankins

PRAISE MATTERS

Praise unlocks heaven's portals;
Praise causes doubts to cease;
Praise brings precious blessings;
Praise leaves the sweetest peace.

Praise breaks all bands asunder;
Praise sets the captives free;
Praise lightens every burden;
Praise is the master key.

Praise changes circumstances;
Praise establishes the heart;
When praise becomes perpetual,
Praise is a Holy Art.[3]

Frances Metcalfe

Exodus 15:1b, 2

"I will sing to the LORD, for he has triumphed gloriously... The LORD is my strength and my song; he has given me victory. This is my God, and I will praise him—my father's God, and I will exalt him!" (NLT)

Verse 2: The LORD is my strong defender; he is the one who has saved me. He is my God, and I will praise him... I will sing about his greatness. (GNT)

Exodus 15:11

Who is like You, O Lord, among the gods? Who is like You, glorious in holiness, awesome in splendor, doing wonders? (AMPC)

Deuteronomy 10:21

He alone is your God, the only one who is worthy of your praise... (NLT)

Deuteronomy 32:3–4

"For I will proclaim the name of *ADONAI*. Come, declare the greatness of our God! The Rock! His work is perfect, for all his ways are just. A trustworthy God who does no wrong..." (CJB)

2 Samuel 22:47

"The LORD lives! Blessed be my Rock! Let God be exalted, the Rock of my salvation!" (NKJV)

1 Chronicles 16:8–10, 12

O give thanks to the Lord, call on His name; make known His doings among the peoples! Sing to Him, sing praises to Him; meditate on and talk of all His wondrous works and devoutly praise them! Glory in His holy name; let the hearts of those rejoice who seek the Lord! ... [Earnestly] remember the marvelous deeds which He has done, His miracles... (AMPC)

1 Chronicles 16:25a, 27–29, 31, 34, 36b

Great is the Lord! He is most worthy of praise! ... Honor and majesty surround him; strength and joy fill his dwelling. O nations of the world, recognize the LORD, recognize that the LORD is glorious and strong. Give to the LORD the glory he deserves! Bring your offering and come into his presence. Worship the LORD in all his holy splendor... Let the heavens be glad, and the earth rejoice! Tell all the nations, "The LORD reigns!"... Give thanks to the LORD, for he is good! His faithful love endures forever... And all the people shouted, "Amen!" and praised the LORD. (NLT)

Verse 31: So let heaven rejoice, let earth be jubilant, and pass the word among the nations, "GOD reigns!" (MSG)

1 Chronicles 29:10b–13

"Blessed are You, LORD God of Israel, our Father, forever and ever. Yours, O LORD, is the greatness, the power and the glory, the victory and the majesty; for all that is in heaven and in earth is Yours; Yours is the kingdom, O LORD, and You are exalted as head over all. Both riches and honor come from You, and You reign over all. In Your hand is power and might; in Your hand it is to make great and to give strength to all. Now therefore, our God, we thank You and praise Your glorious name." (NKJV)

Nehemiah 8:10b

"And be not grieved and depressed, for the joy of the Lord is your strength and stronghold." (AMPC)

Nehemiah 9:5

"…Stand up and bless the LORD your God forever and ever! Blessed be Your glorious name, which is exalted above all blessing and praise!" (NKJV)

"…Stand up and praise the Lord your God, for he lives from everlasting to everlasting. Praise his glorious name! It is far greater than we can think or say." (TLB)

Job 8:21

He will yet fill your mouth with laughing, and your lips with rejoicing. (NKJV)

Psalm 5:11

But let all those who take refuge and put their trust in You rejoice; let them ever sing and shout for joy, because You make a covering over them and defend them; let those also who love Your name be joyful in You and be in high spirits. (AMPC)

Psalm 7:17

I will praise the LORD according to His righteousness, and will sing praise to the name of the LORD Most High. (NKJV)

Oh, how grateful and thankful I am to the Lord because he is so good. I will sing praise to the name of the Lord who is above all lords. (TLB)

Psalm 8:1

O Lord our God, the majesty and glory of your name fills all the earth and overflows the heavens. (TLB)

Psalm 9:1–2

I'm thanking you, GOD, from a full heart, I'm writing the book on your wonders. I'm whistling, laughing, and jumping for joy; I'm singing your song, High God. (MSG)

I will praise you, LORD, with all my heart; I will tell of all the marvelous things you have done. I will be filled with joy because of you. I will sing praises to your name, O Most High. (NLT)

Psalm 9:11

Sing praises to the LORD, who dwells in Zion! Declare His deeds among the people. (NKJV)

Psalm 13:6

I will sing to the Lord, because He has dealt bountifully with me. (AMPC)

...because he gives me even more than I need. (CJB)

...because he is good to me. (NLT)

...because he has blessed me so richly. (TLB)

Psalm 18:3

I will call upon the LORD, who is worthy to be praised; so shall I be saved from my enemies. (NKJV)

Psalm 18:46

The LORD lives! Praise be to my Rock! Exalted be God my Savior! (NIV)

God is alive! Praise him who is the great rock of protection. (TLB)

Psalm 18:49

Therefore will I give thanks and extol You, O Lord, among the nations, and sing praises to Your name. (AMPC)

Psalm 21:13

Be exalted, O Lᴏʀᴅ, in Your own strength! We will sing and praise Your power. (NKJV)

Rise up, O Lᴏʀᴅ, in all your power. With music and singing we celebrate your mighty acts. (NLT)

Psalm 22:3

But You are holy, enthroned in the praises of Israel. (NKJV)

Psalm 22:22–23a

I will declare Your name to my brethren; in the midst of the congregation I will praise You. You who fear (revere and worship) the Lord, praise Him! (AMPC)

Psalm 27:6b

I'm headed for his place to offer anthems that will raise the roof! Already I'm singing God-songs; I'm making music to Gᴏᴅ. (MSG)

Therefore I will offer sacrifices of joy *("joyous shouts"* –NKJV text note*)* in His tabernacle; I will sing, yes, I will sing praises to the LORD. (NKJV)

Psalm 28:7

The LORD is my strength and my shield; my heart trusted in Him, and I am helped; therefore my heart greatly rejoices, and with my song I will praise Him. (NKJV)

He is my strength, my shield from every danger. I trusted in him, and he helped me. Joy rises in my heart until I burst out in songs of praise to him. (TLB)

Psalm 29:2

Give unto the LORD the glory due to His name; worship the LORD in the beauty of holiness. (NKJV)

Psalm 30:4

Sing praise to the LORD, you saints of His, and give thanks at the remembrance of His holy name. (NKJV)

Psalm 30:12

To the end that my tongue and my heart and everything glorious within me may sing praise to You and not be silent. O Lord my God, I will give thanks to You forever. (AMPC)

I'm about to burst with song; I can't keep quiet about you. God, my God, I can't thank you enough. (MSG)

Psalm 31:7

I will be glad and rejoice in Your mercy and steadfast love, because you have seen my affliction, You have taken note of my life's distresses… (AMPC)

Psalm 32:11

Be glad in the LORD and rejoice, you righteous; and shout for joy, all you upright in heart! (NKJV)

Psalm 33:1–3

Rejoice in the LORD, O you righteous! For praise from the upright is beautiful. Praise the LORD with the harp; make melody to Him with an instrument of ten strings. Sing to Him a new song; play skillfully with a shout of joy. (NKJV)

Psalm 34:1–3

I will bless the LORD at all times; His praise shall continually be in my mouth. My soul shall make its boast in the LORD; the humble shall hear of it and be glad. Oh, magnify the LORD with me, and let us exalt His name together. (NKJV)

I will praise the Lord no matter what happens. I will constantly speak of his glories and grace. I will boast of all his kindness to me. Let all who are discouraged take heart. Let us praise the Lord together, and exalt his name. (TLB)

Lord! I'm bursting with joy over what you've done for me! My lips are full of perpetual praise. I'm boasting of you and all your works, so let all who are discouraged take heart. Join me, everyone! Let's praise the Lord together. Let's make him famous! Let's make his name glorious to all. (TPT)

Psalm 35:9–10a

But let me run loose and free, celebrating GOD's great work. Every bone in my body laughing, singing, "GOD, there's no one like you." (MSG)

Then my soul will rejoice in the LORD and delight in his salvation. My whole being will exclaim, "Who is like you, O LORD?" (NIV)

Verse10a: With every bone in my body I will praise him: "LORD, who can compare with you?" (NLT)

Psalm 35:18

I will give You thanks in the great assembly; I will praise You among a mighty throng. (AMPC)

Psalm 35:27–28

Let them shout for joy and be glad, who favor my righteous cause; and let them say continually, "Let the LORD be magnified, who has pleasure in the prosperity of His servant." And my tongue shall speak of Your righteousness and of Your praise all the day long. (NKJV)

Psalm 40:3

He has given me a new song to sing, a hymn of praise to our God. Many will see what he has done and be amazed. They will put their trust in the LORD. (NLT)

Psalm 40:5

O Lord my God, many and many a time you have done great miracles for us, and we are ever in your thoughts. Who else can do such glorious things? No one else can be compared with you. There isn't time to tell of all your wonderful deeds. (TLB)

O Lord, our God, no one can compare with you. Such wonderful works and miracles are all found with you! And you think of us all the time with your countless expressions of love—far exceeding our expectations! (TPT)

Psalm 40:16

Let all those who seek You rejoice and be glad in You; let such as love Your salvation say continually, "The LORD be magnified!" (NKJV)

Psalm 42:11

Why are you down in the dumps, dear soul? Why are you crying the blues? Fix my eyes on God—soon I'll be praising again. He puts a smile on my face. He's my God. (MSG)

Why am I discouraged? Why is my heart so sad? I will put my hope in God! I will praise him again—my Savior and my God! (NLT)

"When life is hardest, the Lord God is still to be praised. It is our only lifeline, our best hope to keep fear from festerin'."[4]

Psalm 44:8

"O God, we give glory to you all day long and constantly praise your name." (NLT)

My constant boast is God. I can never thank you enough. (TLB)

Psalm 47:1–2

Oh, clap your hands, all you peoples! Shout to God with the voice of triumph! For the LORD Most High is awesome; He is a great King over all the earth. (NKJV)

Come, everyone, and clap for joy! Shout triumphant praises to the Lord! For the Lord, the God above all gods, is awesome beyond words; he is the great King of all the earth. (TLB)

Psalm 47:6–7

Sing songs to God, sing out! Sing to our King, sing praise! He's Lord over earth, so sing your best songs to God. (MSG)

Sing out your praises to our God, our King. Yes, sing your highest praises to our King, the King of all the earth. Sing thoughtful praises! (TLB)

Psalm 48:1

Great is the LORD, and most worthy of praise, in the city of our God, his holy mountain. (NIV)

Psalm 48:10

As your name deserves, O God, you will be praised to the ends of the earth. (NLT)

Psalm 50:23a

He who brings an offering of praise and thanksgiving honors and glorifies Me... (AMPC)

Psalm 51:15

O Lord, open my lips, and my mouth will declare Your praise. (MEV)

Psalm 52:11(9)

I will praise you forever for what you have done, and I will put my hope in your name; for this is what is good in the presence of your faithful. (CJB)

Psalm 54:6

I will freely sacrifice to You; I will praise Your name, O Lord, for it is good. (NKJV)

Psalm 56:9b–10a

This one thing I know: God is for me! I am trusting God—oh praise his promises! (TLB)

Psalm 57:7, 9–11

My heart is fixed, O God, my heart is steadfast and confident! I will sing and make melody... I will praise and give thanks to You, O Lord, among the peoples; I will sing praises to You among the nations. For Your mercy and loving-kindness are great, reaching to the heavens, and Your truth and faithfulness to the clouds. Be exalted, O God, above the heavens; let Your glory be over all the earth. (AMPC)

Psalm 59:16–17

But as for me, I will sing about your power. Each morning I will sing with joy about your unfailing love. For you have been my refuge, a place of safety when I am in distress. O my Strength, to you I sing praises, for you, O God, are my refuge, the God who shows me unfailing love. (NLT)

Psalm 63:3–5

Your unfailing love is better than life itself; how I praise you! I will praise you as long as I live, lifting up my hands to you in prayer. You satisfy me more than the richest feast. I will praise you with songs of joy. (NLT)

Psalm 66:1–3a, 4

Make a joyful shout to God, all the earth! Sing out the honor of His name; make His praise glorious. Say to God, "How awesome are Your works! … All the earth shall worship You and sing praises to You; they shall sing praises to Your name." (NKJV)

Psalm 66:8

Oh, bless our God, you people, and make the voice of His praise to be heard. (MEV)

Let the whole world bless our God and loudly sing his praises. (NLT)

Psalm 67:3

Let the peoples praise You, O God; let all the peoples praise You. (NKJV)

Psalm 68:3–4

But let the godly rejoice. Let them be glad in God's presence. Let them be filled with joy. Sing praises to God and to his name! Sing loud praises to him who rides the clouds. His name is the LORD—rejoice in his presence! (NLT)

Psalm 68:19

Blessed be the Lord, who daily loads us with benefits, the God of our salvation! (NKJV)

Psalm 69:30

Let me shout God's name with a praising song, let me tell his greatness in a prayer of thanks. (MSG)

I will praise the name of God with a song, and will magnify Him with thanksgiving. (NKJV)

Psalm 70:4

But may all those who search for you be filled with joy and gladness in you. May those who love your salvation repeatedly shout, "God is great!" (NLT)

Psalm 71:8

Just as each day brims with your beauty, my mouth brims with praise. (MSG)

Let my mouth be filled with Your praise and with Your glory all the day. (NKJV)

All day long I'll praise and honor you, O God, for all that you have done for me. (TLB)

Psalm 71:14–15

But I will hope continually, and will praise You yet more and more. My mouth shall tell of Your righteousness and Your salvation all the day, for I do not know their limits. (NKJV)

I will keep on expecting you to help me. I praise you more and more. I cannot count the times when you have faithfully rescued me from danger. I will tell everyone how good you are, and of your constant daily care. (TLB)

Psalm 71:23

I will shout for joy and sing your praises, for you have ransomed me. (NLT)

Psalm 72:18–19

Praise the LORD God, the God of Israel, who alone does such wonderful things. Praise his glorious name forever! Let the whole earth be filled with his glory. Amen and amen! (NLT)

Psalm 75:1

We thank you, God, we thank you—your Name is our favorite word; your mighty works are all we talk about. (MSG)

We thank you, O God! We give thanks because you are near. People everywhere tell of your wonderful deeds. (NLT)

Psalm 77:13b–14a

Who is so great a God as our God? You are the God who does wonders. (NKJV)

Psalm 79:13

Then we, your people, the ones you love and care for, will thank you over and over and over. We'll tell everyone we meet how wonderful you are, how praiseworthy you are! (MSG)

So we, Your people and sheep of Your pasture, will give You thanks forever; we will show forth Your praise to all generations. (NKJV)

Psalm 86:10, 12–13a

For You are great and work wonders! You alone are God... I will confess and praise You, O Lord my God, with my whole (united) heart; and I will glorify Your name forevermore. For great is Your mercy and loving-kindness toward me... (AMPC)

For you are great and perform wonderful deeds. You alone are God... With all my heart I will praise you, O Lord my God. I will give glory to your name forever, for your love for me is very great. (NLT)

Psalm 89:1

I will sing of the mercies of the LORD forever; with my mouth will I make known Your faithfulness to all generations. (NKJV)

Verses 1–2: Forever and ever I will sing about the tender kindness of the Lord! Young and old shall hear about your blessings. Your love and kindness are forever; your truth is as enduring as the heavens. (TLB)

Psalm 89:52

Blessed be God forever and always! Yes. Oh, yes. (MSG)

Praise the LORD forever! Amen and amen! (NLT)

Psalm 92:1–2, 4–5a

What a beautiful thing, GOD, to give thanks, to sing an anthem to you, the High God! To announce your love each daybreak, sing your faithful presence all through the night... You made me so happy, GOD. I saw your work and I shouted for joy. How magnificent your work, GOD! (MSG)

It is good to give thanks to the LORD, and to sing praises to Your name, O Most High; to declare Your lovingkindness in the morning, and Your faithfulness every night... For You, LORD, have made me glad through Your work; I will triumph in the works of Your hands. O LORD, how great are Your works! (NKJV)

It's so enjoyable to come before you with uncontainable praises spilling from our hearts! How we love to sing our praises over and over to you, to the matchless God, high and exalted over all! At each and every sunrise we will be thanking you for your kindness and your love. As the sun sets and all through the night, we will keep proclaiming, "You are so faithful!"... No wonder I'm so glad; I can't keep it in! Lord, I'm shouting with glee over all you've done, for all you've done for me: what mighty miracles and your power at work—just to name a few. (TPT)

Psalm 95:1–3

Oh come, let us sing to the LORD! Let us shout joyfully to the Rock of our salvation. Let us come before His presence with thanksgiving; let us shout joyfully to Him with psalms. For the LORD is the great God, and the great King above all gods. (NKJV)

Psalm 95:6

Oh come, let us worship and bow down, let us kneel before the Lord our Maker [in reverent praise and supplication]. (AMPC)

Psalm 96:1–4a

Oh, sing to the LORD a new song! Sing to the LORD, all the earth. Sing to the LORD, bless His name; proclaim the good news of His salvation from day to day. Declare His glory among the nations, His wonders among all peoples. For the LORD is great and greatly to be praised... (NKJV)

Psalm 97:12

May all who are godly rejoice in the LORD and praise his holy name! (NLT)

Psalm 98:1a, 4, 6b

Sing to GOD a brand-new song. He's made a world of wonders! ... Shout your praises to GOD, everybody! Let loose and sing! Strike up the band! ... Fill the air with praises to King GOD. (MSG)

Oh, sing to the LORD a new song! For He has done marvelous things... Shout joyfully to the LORD, all the earth; break forth in song, rejoice, and sing praises… Shout joyfully before the Lord, the King. (NKJV)

Psalm 100

Shout with joy to the Lord, all the earth! Worship the Lord with gladness. Come before him, singing with joy. Acknowledge that the Lord is God! He made us, and we are his. We are his people, the sheep of his pasture. Enter his gates with thanksgiving; go into his courts with praise. Give thanks to him and praise his name. For the Lord is good. His unfailing love continues forever, and his faithfulness continues to each generation. (NLT)

Psalm 101:1

I will sing of your love and justice, Lord. I will praise you with songs. (NLT)

Psalm 103:1–5

Bless (affectionately, gratefully praise) the Lord, O my soul; and all that is [deepest] within me, bless His holy name! Bless (affectionately, gratefully praise) the Lord, O my soul, and forget not [one of] all His benefits—Who forgives [every one of] all your iniquities, Who heals [each one of] all your diseases, Who redeems your life from the pit and corruption, Who beautifies, dignifies, and crowns you with loving-kindness and tender mercy; Who satisfies your mouth [your necessity and desire at your personal age and situation] with good so that your youth, renewed, is like the eagle's [strong, overcoming, soaring]! (AMPC)

Let all that I am praise the LORD; with my whole heart, I will praise his holy name. Let all that I am praise the LORD; may I never forget the good things he does for me. He forgives all my sins and heals all my diseases. He redeems me from death and crowns me with love and tender mercies. He fills my life with good things. My youth is renewed like the eagle's! (NLT)

Psalm 104:1–2

Everything I am will praise and bless the Lord! O Lord, my God, your greatness takes my breath away, overwhelming me by your majesty, beauty, and splendor! You wrap yourself with a shimmering, glistening light. You wear sunshine like a garment of glory. You stretch out the starry skies like a tapestry. (TPT)

Psalm 104:33-34, 35b

I will sing to the LORD as long as I live; I will sing praise to my God while I have my being. May my meditation be sweet to Him; I will be glad in the LORD... Bless the Lord, O my soul! Praise the LORD! (NKJV)

I will sing my song to the Lord as long as I live! Every day I will sing my praises to God. May you be pleased with every sweet thought I have about you, for you are the source of my joy and gladness... I will keep on praising you, my Lord, with all that is within me. My joyous, blissful shouts of "Hallelujah" are all because of you! (TPT)

Psalm 105:1–3

Oh, give thanks to the LORD! Call upon His name; make known His deeds among the peoples! Sing to Him, sing psalms to Him; talk of all His wondrous works! Glory in His holy name; let the hearts of those rejoice who seek the LORD! (NKJV)

Psalm 106:1–2

Hallelujah! Thank you, Lord! How good you are! Your love for us continues on forever. Who can ever list the glorious miracles of God? Who can ever praise him half enough? (TLB)

Psalm 107:1–2, 8

Say thank you to the Lord for being so good, for always being so loving and kind. Has the Lord redeemed you? Then speak out! Tell others he has saved you from your enemies... Oh, that these men would praise the Lord for his lovingkindness, and for all of his wonderful deeds! (TLB)

Verse 8: So thank GOD for his marvelous love, for his miracle mercy to the children he loves. (MSG)

Psalm 107:21–22, 43

Let them praise the LORD for his great love and for the wonderful things he has done for them. Let them offer sacrifices of thanksgiving and sing joyfully about his glorious acts... They will see in our history the faithful love of the Lord. (NLT)

Verse 43: Think about the lovingkindness of the Lord! (TLB)

Psalm 108:1–5

My heart, O God, is focused and determined, all because of you. Now I can sing my song with passionate praises! Awake, O my soul, with the music of his splendor. Arise, my soul, and sing his praises! I will awaken the dawn with my worship, greeting the daybreak with my songs… Wherever I go, I will thank you. All the nations will hear my praise songs to you. Your love is so extravagant, it reaches higher than the heavens! Your faithfulness is so astonishing, it stretches to the skies! Lord God, be exalted as you soar throughout the heavens. May your shining glory be seen high above all the earth! (TPT)

Psalm 109:30

But I will give repeated thanks to the Lord, praising Him to everyone. (NLT)

> Thanksgiving throws the door open wide;
> praise keeps it open.
>
> **E.W. Kenyon**

Psalm 111:1–4, 10c

Praise the Lord! I will thank the Lord with all my heart as I meet with his godly people. How amazing are the deeds of the Lord! All who delight in him should ponder them. Everything he does reveals his glory and majesty. His righteousness never fails. He causes us to remember his wonderful works. How gracious and merciful is our Lord! … Praise him forever! (NLT)

Psalm 113:1–3

Hallelujah! You who serve GOD, praise GOD! Just to speak his name is praise! Just to remember GOD is a blessing—now and tomorrow and always. From east to west, from dawn to dusk, keep lifting all your praises to GOD! (MSG)

Praise the LORD! Praise, O servants of the LORD, praise the name of the LORD! Blessed be the name of the LORD from this time forth and forevermore! From the rising of the sun to its going down the LORD's name is to be praised. (NKJV)

Psalm 115:18

But we will bless the LORD from this time forth and forevermore. Praise the LORD! (NKJV)

Psalm 116:17

I will offer to You the sacrifice of thanksgiving, and will call upon the name of the LORD. (NKJV)

Psalm 117:1–2

O praise the Lord, all you nations! Praise Him, all you people! For His mercy and loving-kindness are great toward us, and the truth and faithfulness of the Lord endure forever. Praise the Lord! (Hallelujah!) (AMPC)

Psalm 118:1

O give thanks to the Lord, for He is good; for His mercy and loving-kindness endure forever! (AMPC)

Keep on giving your thanks to God, for he is so good! His constant, tender love lasts forever! (TPT)

Psalm 118:21

I will confess, praise, and give thanks to You, for You have heard and answered me; and You have become my Salvation and Deliverer. (AMPC)

I thank you for answering my prayer and giving me victory. (NLT)

Psalm 118:24

This is the day the LORD has made, we will rejoice and be glad in it. (NKJV)

Psalm 118:28–29

You're my God, and I thank you. O my God, I lift high your praise. Thank GOD—he's so good. His love never quits. (MSG)

You are my God, and I will praise you! You are my God, and I will exalt you! Give thanks to the LORD, for he is good! His faithful love endures forever. (NLT)

Psalm 119:162

I rejoice in your word like one who discovers a great treasure. (NLT)

Your promises are the source of my bubbling joy; the revelation of your Word thrills me like one who has discovered hidden treasure. (TPT)

Psalm 126:2a, 3

Then our mouth was filled with laughter, and our tongue with singing… The LORD has done great things for us, and we are glad. (NKJV)

Psalm 134:2

Lift up holy hands in prayer, and praise the Lord. (NLT)

Psalm 135:1, 3

Hallelujah! Praise the name of GOD, praise the works of GOD… Shout "Hallelujah!" because GOD's so good, sing anthems to his beautiful name. (MSG)

Verse 3: Praise the Lord! For the Lord is good; sing praises to His name, for He is gracious and lovely. (AMPC)

Psalm 136:26

Oh, give thanks to the God of heaven! For His mercy endures forever. (NKJV)

Psalm 138:1–2

Thank you! Everything in me says "Thank you!" Angels listen as I sing my thanks. I kneel in worship... and say it again: "Thank you!" Thank you for your love, thank you for your faithfulness; most holy is your name, most holy is your Word. (MSG)

Psalm 138:5

Yes...sing of the ways of the Lord and joyfully celebrate His mighty acts, for great is the glory of the Lord. (AMPC)

Psalm 139:13–15

For you fashioned my inmost being, you knit me together in my mother's womb. I thank you because I am awesomely made, wonderfully; your works are wonders—I know this very well. My bones were not hidden from you when I was being made in secret, intricately woven in the depths of the earth. (CJB)

Oh yes, you shaped me first inside, then out; you formed me in my mother's womb. I thank you, High God—you're breathtaking! Body and soul, I am marvelously made! I worship in adoration—what a creation! You know me inside and out, you know every bone in my body; you know exactly how I was made, bit by bit, how I was sculpted from nothing into something. (MSG)

For You formed my inward parts; You covered me in my mother's womb. I will praise You, for I am fearfully and wonderfully made; marvelous are Your works, and that my soul knows very well. My frame was not hidden from You, when I was made in secret, and skillfully wrought in the lowest parts of the earth. (NKJV)

You made all the delicate, inner parts of my body, and knit them together in my mother's womb. Thank you for making me so wonderfully complex! It is amazing to think about. Your workmanship is marvelous—and how well I know it. You were there while I was being formed in utter seclusion! (TLB)

Verse 15: My frame was not hidden from You when I was being formed in secret [and] intricately and curiously wrought [as if embroidered with various colors] in the depths of the earth... (AMPC)

Psalm 145:1–12

I will praise you, my God and King, and bless your name each day and forever. Great is Jehovah! Greatly praise him! His greatness is beyond discovery! Let each generation tell its children what glorious things he does. I will meditate about your glory, splendor, majesty and miracles. Your awe-inspiring deeds shall be on every tongue; I will proclaim your greatness. Everyone will tell about how good you are, and sing about your righteousness. Jehovah is kind and merciful, slow to get angry, full of love. He is good to everyone, and his compassion is intertwined with everything he does. All living things shall thank you, Lord, and your people will bless you. They will talk together about the glory of your kingdom and mention examples of your power. They will tell about your miracles and about the majesty and glory of your reign. (TLB)

Psalm 145:21

My mouth is filled with God's praise. Let everything living bless him, bless his holy name from now to eternity! (MSG)

I will praise the Lord, and may everyone on earth bless his holy name forever and ever. (NLT)

Psalm 146:1–2

Praise the Lord! Praise the Lord, O my soul! While I live I will praise the Lord; I will sing praises to my God while I have my being. (NKJV)

Psalm 147:1

Praise the Lord! For it is good to sing praises to our God, for He is gracious and lovely; praise is becoming and appropriate. (AMPC)

Praise the LORD. How good it is to sing praises to our God, how pleasant and fitting to praise him! (NIV)

Psalm 148:13, 14b

Let them praise the name of the LORD, for His name alone is exalted; His glory is above the earth and heaven... Praise the LORD! (NKJV)

Psalm 149:1, 3, 5–6a

Praise the LORD! Sing to the LORD a new song, and His praise in the assembly of saints... Let them praise His name with the dance; let them sing praises to Him with the timbrel and harp... Let the saints be joyful in glory; let them sing aloud on their beds. Let the high praises of God be in their mouth... (NKJV)

Psalm 150

Hallelujah! Praise God in his holy house of worship, praise him under the open skies; praise him for his acts of power, praise him for his magnificent greatness; praise with a blast on the trumpet, praise by strumming soft strings; praise him with castanets and dance, praise him with banjo and flute; praise him with cymbals and a big bass drum, praise him with fiddles and mandolin. Let every living, breathing creature praise GOD! Hallelujah! (MSG)

Praise the LORD! Praise God in His sanctuary; praise Him in His mighty firmament! Praise Him for His mighty acts; praise

Him according to His excellent greatness! Praise Him with the sound of the trumpet; praise Him with the lute and harp! Praise Him with the timbrel and dance; praise Him with stringed instruments and flutes! Praise Him with loud cymbals; praise Him with clashing cymbals! Let everything that has breath praise the LORD. Praise the LORD! (NKJV)

Isaiah 6:3

…"Holy, holy, holy is the LORD Almighty; the whole earth is full of his glory." (NIV)

Isaiah 12:4–5

In that wonderful day you will sing: "Thank the LORD! Praise his name! Tell the nations what he has done. Let them know how mighty he is! Sing to the LORD, for he has done wonderful things. Make known his praise around the world." (NLT)

Verse 5: Sing praises to the Lord, for He has done excellent things [gloriously]; let this be made known to all the earth. (AMPC)

Isaiah 25:1

O Lord, You are my God; I will exalt You, I will praise Your name, for You have done wonderful things, even purposes planned of old [and fulfilled] in faithfulness and truth. (AMPC)

Isaiah 49:13

Sing, heaven! Rejoice, earth! Break out in song, you mountains! For *Adonai* is comforting his people, having mercy on his own who have suffered. (CJB)

Shout for joy, you heavens; rejoice, you earth; burst into song, you mountains! For the Lord comforts his people and will have compassion on his afflicted ones. (NIV)

Isaiah 61:10

I will greatly rejoice in the Lord, my soul shall be joyful in my God; for He has clothed me with the garments of salvation, He has covered me with the robe of righteousness... (NKJV)

Isaiah 63:7

I will tell of the Lord's unfailing love. I will praise the Lord for all he has done. (NLT)

Jeremiah 32:17

Alas, Lord God! Behold, You have made the heavens and the earth by Your great power and by your outstretched arm! There is nothing too hard or too wonderful for You. (AMPC)

Lamentations 3:22–23

The faithful love of the Lord never ends! His mercies never cease. Great is his faithfulness; his mercies begin afresh each morning. (NLT)

Daniel 2:20

...Blessed be the name of God forever and ever! For wisdom and might are His! (AMPC)

Joel 2:21

Fear not, my people; be glad now and rejoice, for he has done amazing things for you. (TLB)

Habakkuk 3:18

Yet I will rejoice in the LORD, I will joy in the God of my salvation. (NKJV)

> Praise is powerful!
> Praise is putting your faith in action.
>
> **Joel Osteen**

Luke 1:46–47

"My soul magnifies (*"declares the greatness of"* —NKJV text note) the Lord, and my spirit has rejoiced in God my Savior!" (NKJV)

Luke 19:37–38

... the whole multitude of the disciples began to rejoice and praise God with a loud voice for all the mighty works they had seen, saying: '"*Blessed is the King who comes in the name of the* LORD*!* 'Peace in heaven and glory in the highest!" (NKJV)

Luke 24:53

And they were continually in the temple celebrating with praises and blessing and extolling God. Amen (so be it). (AMPC)

Acts 3:8

...walking back and forth, dancing and praising God. (MSG)

So he, leaping up, stood and walked and entered the temple with them—walking, leaping, and praising God. (NKJV)

PRAISE AT MIDNIGHT

Acts 16:25–26

"And at midnight Paul and Silas prayed, and sang praises unto God: and the prisoners heard them. And suddenly there was a great earthquake, so that the foundations of the prison were shaken: and immediately all the doors were opened, and everyone's bands were loosed." (KJV)

The darkness still is deep'ning,
O tried and weary heart,
No rift of morning brightness
Bids midnight gloom depart;
The prison walls surround thee,
No human help is nigh,
But blest is the assurance
Thy Savior reigns on high.

When shadowed in the darkness,
And pressed by every foe,
Then let your gladdest carols
And sweetest anthems flow;
The praise so sweet to Jesus,
The "sacrifice of praise,"
Is when no earthly sunshine
Pours forth its cheering rays.

'Tis then your song is wafted
All human heights above,
And mingles with the angels',
In realms of perfect love;
'Tis then the God of glory
Makes Satan fear and flee,
And sends a mighty earthquake
To set His ransomed free.

'Tis easy when the morning
Appears at last to view,
To praise the strong Redeemer,
Who burst the bondage through.
But 'tis the praise at midnight
That gives the foe alarm,
That glorifies thy Savior,
And bares His strong right arm.

A conqueror thou wouldst be?
Yea, more than conqueror thou,
If thou wilt shout in triumph,
And claim the victory now;
The prison doors will open,
The dungeon gleam with light,
And sin-chained souls around thee
Shall see Jehovah's might.[5]

Romans 4:20

...but he grew strong and was empowered by faith as he gave praise and glory to God. (AMPC)

Romans 8:31

What then shall we say to these things? If God is for us, who can be against us? (NKJV)

Romans 11:33–36

O the depth of the riches and wisdom and knowledge of God! How unsearchable are His judgments and unfathomable are His ways! For who has known the mind of the Lord? Or who has become His counselor? Or who has first given to Him, and it shall be repaid to him? For from Him and through Him and to Him are all things. To Him be glory forever! Amen. (MEV)

Romans 12:12

Rejoice and exult in hope. (AMPC)

1 Corinthians 15:57

But thanks be to God, who gives us the victory through our Lord Jesus Christ. (NKJV)

2 Corinthians 1:3

Praised be God, Father of our Lord Yeshua the Messiah, compassionate Father, God of all encouragement and comfort. (CJB)

What a wonderful God we have—he is the Father of our Lord Jesus Christ, the source of every mercy, and the one who wonderfully comforts and strengthens us in our hardships and trials. (TLB)

2 Corinthians 2:14

But thanks be to God, Who in Christ always leads us in triumph [as trophies of Christ's victory]... (AMPC)

Wherever I go, thank God, He makes my life a constant pageant of triumph in Christ. (MOF)

2 Corinthians 9:15

Now thanks be to God for His Gift, [precious] beyond telling [His indescribable, inexpressible, free Gift]! (AMPC)

Thank God for his Son—his Gift too wonderful for words. (TLB)

2 Corinthians 10:17

But "he who glories, let him glory in the Lord." (NKJV)

Galatians 1:5

All glory to God forever and ever! Amen. (NLT)

Ephesians 1:6

So we praise God for the glorious grace he has poured out on us who belong to his dear Son. (NLT)

Ephesians 5:4b

...but instead voice your thankfulness [to God]. (AMPC)

Instead, let worship fill your heart and spill out in your words. (TPT)

Ephesians 5:19–20

... singing and making melody in your heart to the Lord, giving thanks always for all things to God the Father in the name of our Lord Jesus Christ... (NKJV)

Verse 19: Sing songs from your hearts to Christ. Sing praises over everything, any excuse for a song to God the Father... (MSG)

Verse 19: Sing and offer praise in your hearts to the Lord. (WEY)

Philippians 3:1

...continue to rejoice that you are in Him. (AMPC)

My beloved ones, don't ever limit your joy or fail to rejoice in the wonderful experience of knowing our Lord Jesus! (TPT)

Philippians 4:4

Rejoice in the Lord always [delight, gladden yourselves in Him]; again I say, Rejoice! (AMPC)

Philippians 4:8b

...And fasten your thoughts on every glorious work of God, praising him always. (TPT)

Colossians 1:3

...continually give thanks to God the Father of our Lord Jesus Christ... (AMPC)

Colossians 1:11–12

...keep going no matter what happens—always full of the joy of the Lord, and always thankful to the Father who has made us fit to share all the wonderful things that belong to those who live in the Kingdom of light. (TLB)

Colossians 2:7c

Let your lives overflow with joy and thanksgiving for all he has done. (TLB)

Colossians 3:15b

And be thankful (appreciative), [giving praise to God always]. (AMPC)

Colossians 3:16c

Sing psalms and hymns and spiritual songs to God with thankful hearts. (NLT)

Colossians 3:17b

And bring your constant praise to God the Father because of what Christ has done for you! (TPT)

1 Thessalonians 5:16, 18

Be happy [in your faith] and rejoice and be glad-hearted continually (always)... Thank [God] in everything [no matter what the circumstances may be, be thankful and give thanks], for this is the will of God for you [who are] in Christ Jesus [the Revealer and Mediator of that will]. (AMPC)

Rejoice always... in everything give thanks; for this is the will of God in Christ Jesus for you. (NKJV)

Hebrews 12:28

...let us be thankful, and so worship God acceptably with reverence and awe... (NIV)

Hebrews 13:15

Therefore by Him let us continually offer the sacrifice of praise to God, that is, the fruit of our lips, giving thanks to His name. (NKJV)

1 Peter 1:3, 6a

All honor to God, the God and Father of our Lord Jesus Christ; for it is his boundless mercy that has given us the privilege of being born again, so that we are now members of God's own family... So be truly glad! (TLB)

Celebrate with praises the God and Father of our Lord Jesus Christ, who has shown us his extravagant mercy... May the thought of this cause you to jump for joy... (TPT)

1 Peter 1:8b

...yet believing, you rejoice with joy inexpressible and full of glory... (NKJV)

1 Peter 2:9b

...proclaim the praises of Him who called you out of darkness into His marvelous light. (NKJV)

1 Peter 4:11b

...that in all things God may be glorified through Jesus Christ, to whom belong the glory and the dominion forever and ever. Amen. (NKJV)

Jude 24-25

Now to Him who is able to keep you from stumbling, and to present you faultless before the presence of His glory with exceeding joy, to God our Savior, Who alone is wise, be glory and majesty, dominion and power, both now and forever. Amen. (NKJV)

Joy is the serious business of heaven.

C.S. Lewis

Revelation 4:6b, 8b–11

In the center and around the throne were four living beings... Day after day and night after night they keep on saying, "Holy, holy, holy is the Lord God Almighty—the one who always was, who is, and who is still to come!" Whenever the living beings give glory and honor and thanks to the one sitting on the throne (the one who lives forever and ever), the twenty-four elders fall down and worship the one sitting on the throne (the one who lives forever and ever). And they lay their crowns before the throne and say, "You are worthy, O Lord our God, to receive glory and honor and power. For you created all things, and they exist because you created what you pleased." (NLT)

Revelation 5:11–14

Then I looked, and I heard the voice of many angels around the throne, the living creatures, and the elders; and the number of them was ten thousand times ten thousand and thousands of thousands, saying with a loud voice: "Worthy is the Lamb who was slain to receive power and riches and wisdom, and strength and honor and glory and blessing!" And every creature which is in heaven and on the earth and under the earth and such as are in the sea, and all that are in them, I heard saying: "Blessing and honor and glory and power be to Him who sits on the throne, and to the Lamb, forever and ever!" Then the four living creatures said, "Amen!" And the twenty-four elders fell down and worshiped Him who lives forever and ever. (NKJV)

Revelation 7:11–12

All the angels were standing in a circle around the throne with the elders and the four living creatures, and they all fell on their faces before the throne and worshiped God, singing: "Amen! Praise and glory, wisdom and thanksgiving, honor, power, and might belong to our God forever and ever! Amen!" (TPT)

Revelation 15:3–4

…Mighty your acts and marvelous, O God, the Sovereign-Strong! Righteous your ways and true, King of the nations! Who can fail to fear you, God, give glory to your Name? Because you and you only are holy, all nations will come and worship you, because they see your judgments are right. (MSG)

And they were singing the song of Moses… and the song of the Lamb: "Great and marvelous are your works, O Lord God, the Almighty. Just and true are your ways, O King of the nations.

Who will not fear you, Lord, and glorify your name? For you alone are holy. All nations will come and worship before you, for your righteous deeds have been revealed." (NLT)

Revelation 19:1

After this I heard what sounded like a mighty shout of a great crowd in heaven, exclaiming, Hallelujah (praise the Lord)! Salvation and glory (splendor and majesty) and power (dominion and authority) [belong] to our God! (AMPC)

Revelation 19:4–7a

Then the twenty-four Elders and the four Living Beings fell down and worshiped God, who was sitting upon the throne, and said, "Amen! Hallelujah! Praise the Lord!" And out of the throne came a voice that said, "Praise our God, all you his servants, small and great, who fear him." Then I heard again what sounded like the shouting of a huge crowd, or like the waves of a hundred oceans crashing on the shore, or like the mighty rolling of great thunder, "Praise the Lord! For the Lord our God, the Almighty, reigns. Let us be glad and rejoice and honor him..." (TLB)

Verses 6-7: And I seemed to hear the voices of a great multitude and the sound of many waters and of loud peals of thunder, which said, "Hallelujah! Because our God the Lord Omnipotent has begun His reign. Let us rejoice and triumph and give Him the glory..." (WEY)

So let's keep on giving
our thanks to God,
for he is so good!
His constant, tender love
lasts forever!

Psalm 118:29 (TPT)

Praise is the pathway to joy.

Personal Praise Notes

Personal Praise Notes

Personal Praise Notes

Personal Praise Notes

Glossary

Bless – *Strong's* H1288: An act of adoration; to salute, praise, thank, congratulate; kneel down, i.e., to speak or receive words of blessing.[5] (Psalm 145:2)

Bless Continually – *Strong's* H8548: Constantly, always, evermore, perpetually; to stretch (out to eternity); permanent, daily, or regular.[6] (Psalm 34:1)

Blessing – *Strong's* G2127, G2129: To speak well of, extol, bless abundantly, invoke a benediction, give thanks.[7] (Revelation 5:13)

Exalted – *Strong's* H7311: To elevate, raise, bring up, exalt, lift up, hold up, extol; to make high and powerful.[8] (Psalm 18:46)

Glad – *Strong's* H8056: Gleeful, (be) joyful, merry (-hearted), rejoicing.[9] (Psalm 32:11)

Glorify – *Strong's* H3513: To make numerous, rich, honorable or great. The English word means, to elevate to celestial glory; to shed radiance and splendor upon; to magnify, adore and exalt.[10] (Psalm 50:23)

Glory – *Strong's* H3519: Weightiness; that which is substantial or heavy; glory, honor, splendor, power, wealth, authority, magnificence, fame, dignity, riches, and excellency.[11] (Isaiah 6:3)

Glory – *Strong's G139:* Honor or glory given to peoples, nations, and individuals; splendor, radiance, and majesty centered in Jesus.[12] (Revelation 4:11)

Joy – *Strong's H1523:* To joy, rejoice, be glad, be joyful; suggests dancing for joy or leaping for joy; to spin around or whirl with intense motion, i.e., like David in 2 Samuel 6:14. [13] (Habakkuk 3:18)

Joyful – *Strong's H8056:* Happy, joyful, cheerful, rejoicing, festive.[14] (Psalm 66:1)

Magnify – *Strong's G3170:* To make (or declare) great, to enlarge, to magnify, to increase, to extol, to show respect, to hold in high esteem.[15] (Luke 1:46)

Praise – *Strong's H1984:* To praise, to thank; rejoice, boast about someone; conveys the idea of speaking or singing about the glories, virtues, or honor of someone or something.[16] (Psalm 135:3)

Praise – *Strong's H8416:* A celebration, a lauding of someone praiseworthy; the praise or exaltation of God; praises, songs of admiration.[17] (Psalm 100:4)

Extreme Praise

See Psalm 150:2 • To "shine, boast, rave, and to celebrate clamorously"…not only "from the silence of awe" but "to songs of joy…" We must be "willing to incorporate the shout of triumph—see Psalm 47:1."[18]

Sing and shout joyfully to the Lord. If we can shout at other public events, surely we can give loud and enthusiastic praise to God, whether with others or by ourselves. Freely shout His praise with all of your heart and strength (Psalms 95:1-2; 98:4-6; 100:1).[19]

Praise – *Strong's G1868:* Commendation, approval, praise—not only for what God does for us, but also for who He is, recognizing His glory.[20] (Ephesians 1:6)

Rejoices – *Strong's H7797:* To rejoice, be glad, be greatly happy.[21] (Psalm 119:162)

Thanks – *Strong's H3034:* To revere or worship with extended hands; to praise, declare the merits of someone.[22] (1 Chronicles 16:8)

Thanks – *Strong's G2168:* To give freely, to be grateful, to express gratitude, to be thankful.[23] (1 Corinthians 15:57)

Thanksgiving – *Strong's H8426:* *(To give)* thanks, thanksgiving, adoration, *(to give)* praise—as to lift or extend one's hands in thanks and praise to God.[24] (Psalm 95:2)

Endnotes

1. Don Gossett. *There's Dynamite in Praise: How to Get Your Prayers Answered, and Then Some.* © 1974 by Whitaker House, pp. 38–39.

2. Ibid., pp. 18–19.

3. James Maloney. *Ladies of Gold*, Vol. 1. © 2011 by Answering the Cry Publications, pp. 233–234.

4. Beverly Lewis. *The Wish.* © 2016 by Bethany House Publishing.

5. Carrie Judd Montgomery. *The Life of Praise.* PUBLIC DOMAIN.

6–10. James Strong. *The New Strong's Exhaustive Concordance of the Bible.* © 2010 by Thomas Nelson.

11. Maloney, p. 248.

12–18. Strong. *The New Strong's Exhaustive Concordance of the Bible.*

19. Jack W. Hayford. *The Hayford Bible Handbook.* © 1995 by Thomas Nelson,. p. 743.

20.   "Truth-in-Action ② Cultivating Dynamic Devotion." *New Spirit-Filled Life˚ Bible* (New King James Version). © 2002 by Thomas Nelson, p. 770.

21–25. Strong. *The New Strong's Exhaustive Concordance of the Bible.*

Additional Reading

Gossett, Don. *There's Dynamite in Praise: How to Get Your Prayers Answered and Then Some.* Don Gossett. New Kensington, PA: Whitaker House, 1974.

Gossett, Don. *Praise Avenue.* New Kensington, PA: Whitaker House, 1976, 2012.

Hagin, Kenneth E. *Greater Glory.* Tulsa: RHEMA Bible Church, AKA Kenneth Hagin Ministries, 1999.

Hagin, Kenneth W. *The Untapped Power In Praise,* Tulsa: 1990 RHEMA Bible Church, AKA Kenneth Hagin Ministries, 1990

Maloney, James. *Ladies of Gold, Volume One.* Bloomington, IN: WestBow Press, a Division of Thomas Nelson, 2011.

Montgomery, Carrie Judd. *The Life of Praise, Fourth Edition.* Reprint from the collection of the University of California Libraries, Berkeley, CA.

Wommack, Andrew. *The Effects of Praise.* Colorado Springs: Andrew Wommack Ministries, Inc., published in partnership with Harrison House Publishing, 2008.

For more information or
to purchase copies of this book,
visit the author page for J.M. Smith
at www.bushpublishing.com.

About the Author

Janet Smith and her husband, both in their 70s, responded to a nudge from God in 2018 to "go to a land that I will show you." Not unlike another who received such a Biblical mandate, these lifelong Minnesotans packed up 35 years of marital accumulations—and leaving family, friends, and church, they journeyed to the land of... The Ozarks! Central Missouri! Seriously? Oh, yes, you betcha!

Experiencing the gamut of emotions that such a move from all that is familiar and comfortable brought helped to further Smith's passion for and belief in the power of praise. She loves sharing encouragement with testimonies and scripture verses that empower others with a desire to deepen their relationship with God, discover aspects of God's character that they may not have considered, and cultivate and enjoy a lifestyle of praising the Lord!

Smith and her husband have a uniquely blended family that includes five children and many beautiful, intelligent grandchildren and great-grandchildren.

CPSIA information can be obtained
at www.ICGtesting.com
Printed in the USA
LVHW080806020522
717598LV00021B/430